CW01498188

Original title:
Inlaid Rumors Along the Fae Shelf

Author: Olivia Oja
ISBN HARDBACK: 978-1-80563-329-7
ISBN PAPERBACK: 978-1-80564-850-5

Labyrinth of Luminescent Lies

In the heart where shadows dwell,
Truth and fantasy weave a spell.
Whispers float through the dim-lit maze,
Where hope and despair dance in haze.

Mirrors reflect what we wish to see,
Shimmering paths lead you to me.
Flickering lights will guide your quest,
But beware of the hidden jest.

A flick of a wand, a step in time,
Secrets wrapped in rhythm and rhyme.
Each corner turned, another lie,
Echoing softly, a melancholic sigh.

The heartbeats sync with a ghostly tune,
Silvered stars fall like plumes.
Yet, amidst the gleam of false delight,
Lies lie waiting, shrouded in night.

Courage falters, yet still you roam,
Seeking the truth, longing for home.
In the labyrinth, where fantasies twine,
Will you emerge, or forever entwine?

Secrets of the Adorned Sylvan Arc

Beneath the boughs where the wild things sing,
Nature hides treasures, a wondrous thing.
Glistening petals, jewels in the light,
Masked in the day, revealed in the night.

The arch of branches forms a grand hall,
Echoing whispers, a siren's call.
Each leaf a story, each breeze a song,
Nature's embrace where we all belong.

Footfalls softened by emerald beds,
Dreams curled like ferns in delicate threads.
Magic flows through the air like wine,
As mysteries whisper in ages divine.

In dappled shade, where shadows entwine,
The spirits of the woods so benign.
Seek the path where the faeries play,
And find the secrets that linger and sway.

The archers of fate draw their bows with care,
Guarding the wonder that dances in air.
A flicker of hope in the sylvan arc,
Calls to the dreamers within the dark.

Shadows of Whimsy Beneath the Branch

In the twilight's glow, a dance begins,
Shadows of whimsy twirl on a whim.
Beneath the branches where laughter spills,
A tapestry woven with magical thrills.

Giggling fairies skip through the night,
Chasing the stars, oh, what a sight!
The moon winks down with a knowing grin,
As secrets of joy weave their way in.

Rustling leaves sing sweet lullabies,
Cradling dreams in their sweetened sighs.
Each flicker of light, a story unfolds,
Whispers of whimsy in legends retold.

In every shadow, a character hides,
Awaiting the moment when magic abides.
The pulse of the forest beats strong and free,
Unraveling dreams for the curious to see.

With innocence clinging like dew on the grass,
In the realm of the night, let the echoes pass.
For beneath the branches, in laughter and song,
The shadows of whimsy forever belong.

Whispers of the Tempest's Caress

In the heart of a storm where the wild winds blow,
Thunderous whispers beckon below.
Each crack of lightning reveals the unknown,
A tempest's caress, a magic overgrown.

The clouds bicker softly in colors so bold,
Painting the skies with stories untold.
Rain dances down in an intricate waltz,
A symphony born from nature's pulse.

With every gust, secrets unravel,
Winds of fortune, the paths we travel.
The sea roars fiercely, a lover spurned,
Craving the solace that is often yearned.

In the eye of the storm, a calm resides,
The heart finds peace where awe abides.
Listen close to the thunder's sigh,
In whispers forgotten, a world awry.

From the depths of chaos, clarity gleams,
In the whispering tempest, chase your dreams.
For in every storm, there lies a chance,
To dance with the winds, a dazzling romance.

Chimeras in the Whispering Wind

In twilight's hush, the chimeras blend,
A dance of shadows, where whispers wend.
They flit through forests, both wild and free,
Secrets entwined in their ghostly spree.

With wings of starlight, they soar and dive,
In dreams we find them, forever alive.
A serenade calls from the moonlit sky,
Where tales of wonder and magic lie.

Each breath of wind carries tales untold,
Of creatures that shimmer like silver and gold.
Through ancient trees, they weave their lore,
In the quiet spaces, they linger and soar.

Listen, dear heart, to the night's soft song,
For in every sigh, where the spirits belong,
Is a promise of magic, hidden and bright,
A glimpse of the chimeras in the moonlight.

As the stars converse in the velvet night,
Find solace in dreams, take magical flight.
For if you believe, you might just see,
The wonders that dwell in this land of glee.

Luxembourg Past the Faery Lights

Beyond the rivers, where the faeries dwell,
Luxembourg shines with a mystic spell.
Each lantern glows like a twinkling star,
Guiding the dreamers, both near and far.

The cobbled streets whisper stories old,
Of knights and treasures, of gems untold.
Every corner holds a forgotten delight,
In the gardens of faeries, beneath silver light.

Listen to laughter that dances on air,
The echoes of magic, a wondrous affair.
With each step forward, you'd lose track of time,
In this world where dreams and reality chime.

They weave in and out of the shadows cast,
A tapestry glimmering, built to last.
With mischief and joy, they play and tease,
In Luxembourg's heart, every heart finds ease.

So wander along, let your spirit take flight,
Past faery lights, into the night,
For in every corner, a new tale ignites,
In the enchanting realm of Luxembourg's sights.

The Tapestry of Hidden Paths

In forests deep, where the hidden paths lie,
A tapestry sways 'neath the brightening sky.
Threads of the ancients weave tales of the brave,
In whispers of leaves, their stories they save.

Each step you take on this winding way,
Unravels secrets that beckon to play.
With every shadow that dances around,
A world of wonder is waiting to be found.

The light filters through, painting gold on the ground,
In the stillness of nature, there's magic profound.
Follow the echoes that beckon your heart,
For the journey unfolds as new wonders start.

Through valleys and hills, where time seems to freeze,
You'll find the laughter hidden in the breeze.
A map of enchantment in every new stride,
The tapestry waits—will you turn the tide?

So venture forth, let your spirit ignite,
On this canvas of dreams, in the soft twilight.
For paths may be hidden, yet always they're there,
In the tapestry woven, with love and with care.

Crystals of Insight in Enchanted Groves

In enchanted groves, where the sunlight falls,
Crystals of insight echo through the halls.
Each shimmering fragment a glimpse of the soul,
Reflecting the wisdom that makes us whole.

With whispers of wind, the secrets unfold,
Stories of ages, in whispers retold.
The branches sway gently, a lullaby sweet,
Guiding the wanderers, where shadows retreat.

The fragrance of blossoms, a delicate scent,
Here in this haven, time seems to relent.
Every petal gleams, every leaf is a guide,
In this sanctuary where dreams coincide.

So pause for a moment, in stillness embrace,
Let the crystals of insight illuminate space.
For deep in your heart a new wisdom grows,
In the enchanted groves, where magic flows.

With each breath you take, let your spirit soar,
Beyond the illusions, to life's open door.
For in every grove, every shimmering light,
Lies the gift of vision, profound and bright.

Kisses of Enchantment Upon the Air

In twilight's glow, the whispers dance,
A gentle breeze, a fleeting chance.
With every sigh, a secret shared,
The kiss of magic, hearts ensnared.

Moonlit shadows weave through night,
Each glance a spell, a spark of light.
In tender moments, souls ignite,
Enchanting dreams take glorious flight.

The stars bear witness, soft and bright,
To love's embrace, the purest sight.
In every breath, enchantment lies,
Awakening magic 'neath starlit skies.

Through floral scents and evening's calm,
Each memory wrapped in nature's psalm.
A world where wishes softly dwell,
In kisses sweet, we weave our spell.

So let the night forever sing,
Of heart's delight and the joy they bring.
In whispers soft, our hearts shall share,
The kisses sweet, enchantment rare.

Mystique of the Shimmering Glade

In glade where silver moonlight streams,
Mystique awakens from hidden dreams.
Soft rustling leaves, a gentle sigh,
As echoes hum a lullaby.

The faeries dance on beams of gold,
In every heart, a story told.
Through twilight's veil, the secrets flow,
Where whispers weave and magic grows.

A river's song, a soft embrace,
In nature's heart, we find our place.
With every step, enchantments bloom,
In glimmers bright that chase the gloom.

The flowers nod, their petals bright,
Under the watchful moonlit night.
In shadows deep, the magic calls,
As night unfurls its velvet shawls.

So breathe the air of dreams once spun,
In glade where all our journeys run.
With every step, let wonder play,
In mystique's hold, we long to stay.

The Quill of Enchanted Stories

In ink of night, the quill does trace,
Each tale of wonder, time and space.
With every stroke, a world awakes,
In whispered dreams, the heart remakes.

Upon the page, bright visions soar,
In enchanted lands we yearn for more.
With heroes bold and tales untold,
In every line, magic enfold.

As dragons roar and fairies fly,
The quill weaves spells, emotions tie.
In every drop of ink, a spark,
Illuminating journeys bright and dark.

The stories flow like rivers wide,
Through landscapes vast, where dreams abide.
From parchment leaves to hearts that yearn,
The quill ignites a sacred burn.

So take the quill, let stories grow,
In enchanted realms with endless flow.
For every heart, a tale to share,
With every word, sweet magic's glare.

Elysian Cadences in the Woodland Realm

In woodland realms where echoes play,
Elysian cadences weave their way.
With rustling leaves that sing along,
The earth awake to nature's song.

Beneath the boughs of ancient trees,
A symphony rides the gentle breeze.
The sunbeams dappling soft and rare,
While shadows twirl in vibrant air.

Each brook a whisper, every stone,
Reflects the magic of the known.
With every step, the heart takes flight,
In melodies that crown the night.

The creatures join with joyous cheer,
As twilight calls, inviting near.
In every moment, peace resides,
In woodland magic, the spirit glides.

So linger here, where dreams align,
In elysian rhythms, hearts entwine.
With nature's pulse, let spirits soar,
In woodland realms, forevermore.

Murmurs from the Ether's Edge

Whispers float on softest breeze,
Where shadows weave through ancient trees.
Echoes of the dreams long past,
In twilight's hush, their spell is cast.

Glimmers dance on starlit stream,
A tapestry of thoughts we dream.
Fleeting glimpses of forgotten lore,
In every sigh, we seek much more.

A symphony of night unfolds,
With secrets wrapped in silken folds.
Voices call from realms afar,
In silence, listen, there they are.

The moonlight bathes the world in white,
As shadows whisper tales of night.
A gentle pulse of magic sings,
Unraveling what darkness brings.

In tangled woods, the stories grow,
Each rustle hints at what we know.
Murmurs soft, yet oh so clear,
Awakening the ancients here.

Lacquered Dreams of the Sylvan Realm

In forests deep, where faeries dwell,
The air is thick with magic's spell.
Lacquered dreams on branches lay,
In shafts of light, they drift away.

Petals glisten with morning dew,
Each color bright, a wondrous hue.
Creatures stir in dappled shade,
In whispered tales of silk and jade.

The rivers hum a soothing tune,
Beneath the watchful eyes of moon.
A kingdom rich with charm and grace,
In every nook, a hidden place.

The whispers of the woodland speak,
In quiet tones, they seem to seek.
To unveil what dreams reside,
Within the heart, where hopes collide.

In lacquered dreams, the past is found,
In every wish, the earth is bound.
A story woven through the night,
In sylvan realms, all is delight.

Smoky Hues of the Mysterious Wood

Veils of mist curl through the air,
In smoky hues, the shadows stare.
Beneath the boughs where secrets creep,
The ancient woods, their silence deep.

Soft whispers flit on autumn's breath,
With hints of life and hints of death.
Each rustle tells a tale or two,
Of things unseen, yet felt anew.

The paths unwind like dreams untold,
With fleeting glimmers, faint yet bold.
A heartbeat thumps in nature's thrall,
In the dark, we heed the call.

From smoky hues, the spirits rise,
In quiet night beneath the skies.
A dance of shadows found so near,
Where echoes linger, crystal clear.

The wood reveals both joy and pain,
In every step, its hidden gain.
Among the trees, we learn to see,
The mystery that sets us free.

Silhouette of Secrets in the Twilight Dance

Beneath the sky, where twilight glows,
The silhouette of life bestows.
In shadows cast, the stories weave,
With every breath, the dusk will cleave.

The dance of night begins to stir,
While gentle breezes softly purr.
Each figure sways, a fleeting grace,
In hidden realms, time leaves no trace.

With every turn, a secret spun,
In whispered tales, we come undone.
A fleeting glance, a knowing smile,
As dreams conjoin and hearts compile.

The twilight's cloak, a soft embrace,
In shadows deep, we find our place.
Each movement speaks in silence loud,
A tapestry of night endowed.

With each heartbeat, we twirl and sway,
In twilight's dance, we lose our way.
In silhouette, the world expands,
As twilight whispers, life commands.

Reflections of Mischief on Water's Edge

Beneath the willow's drooping shade,
The whispers of the water played,
With ripples dancing, tales unfold,
Of pixies brave and spirits bold.

A winked eye from the shadowed bank,
Awakens mischief, a prankster's prank,
As stones are skipped with joyous cheer,
And laughter echoes, shimmering clear.

The murmur of the depths below,
Hides secrets only dreamers know,
Where shimmering dreams and shadows blend,
The night concedes, yet does not end.

In twilight's breath, the stories flow,
With every swirl, the currents glow,
And time stands still, a fleeting dance,
As spirits twirl in a merry prance.

So linger here, where water sings,
And playful hearts spread silken wings,
For mischief waits, a friend to call,
In mirrored worlds that weave through all.

The Canvas of Wistful Legends

Upon the breeze, the stories drift,
A tapestry, a splendid gift,
With threads of gold and silver spun,
Each tale, a spark, a fleeting sun.

The colors swirl in vibrant hues,
Of ancient dreams and olden views,
Where knights in armor bravely roam,
And sweethearts weave their tales of home.

Beneath the arch of starlit skies,
The echoes of the past arise,
In twilight's glow, the legends dance,
Inviting hearts to seek romance.

With painted skies as our delight,
We wander through the endless night,
Where every brushstroke tells a tale,
Of hopeful hearts that dared to sail.

So take a seat, and let us spin,
These wondrous tales from deep within,
For on this canvas, life is bright,
And magic stirs in every night.

Faery Flights Through Moonlit Paths

In shadows grand, the faeries glide,
Through silver beams, they swiftly ride,
With wings that shimmer, soft as dreams,
They dance upon the moonlit streams.

The nightingale sings, a gentle tune,
As tiny bells chime with the moon,
And every flower, aglow with light,
Awakens magic in the night.

A flutter here, a whisper there,
The faeries paint the midnight air,
With laughter bright, they chase the stars,
In playful bounds, past Venus and Mars.

Along the paths where echoes play,
In secret glades, they twirl and sway,
With gossamer threads that softly bind,
The world's lost dreams to hearts entwined.

So join their flight through night's embrace,
And follow where they weave their grace,
For in their joy, the heart takes wing,
To dance with faeries and feel their spring.

Songs of the Glimmering Sylphs

In forest deep, where shadows dwell,
The sylphs weave songs, a gentle spell,
With voices soft as fleeting sighs,
They beckon forth the wandering eyes.

Upon the breeze, their laughter flows,
Like streams that shimmer where wildflowers grow,
A symphony of joy and grace,
In harmony, they find their place.

By moonlit glades, they twirl and spin,
With every note, the night begins,
A serenade to calm the heart,
In whispered tones, the magic starts.

So listen close, and hear the call,
Of sylphs who dance and rise and fall,
For in their songs, the world transforms,
A tapestry of love that warms.

With every hymn, a bond is found,
In nature's breath, the heart unbound,
For songs of sylphs, like stars above,
Shine ever bright, a gift of love.

Echoes in the Faery Mist

In the glen where shadows dance,
Whispers ride the evening breeze,
Secrets held in twilight's trance,
Fragmented dreams that time will seize.

Crickets sing a lullaby,
Stars awaken, one by one,
Moonlit paths where fairies fly,
Crafting magic till the dawn.

Softly glows the faery light,
Guiding footsteps through the night,
Echos twirl in silver beams,
Stirring thoughts and gentle dreams.

Laughter ripples through the trees,
Nature holds her breath and waits,
Glimmers set the heart at ease,
As the faery magic bates.

With a sigh, the mist will fade,
Leaving only wonder here,
Every choice a charm that's made,
In the heart where dreams appear.

Veils of Moonlight and Myth

Within the night, the tales unfold,
Veils of silver, soft and bright,
Fables whispered, brave yet bold,
Carried on the wings of night.

Gentle waves of moonlit streams,
Cradle hearts in sweet embrace,
Every shadow holds a dream,
Silent time begins to trace.

Legends spin upon the breeze,
Twirling softly as they flow,
Fleeting thoughts like ancient trees,
Rooted deep in what we know.

Twilight paints the world in hues,
Golden sands beneath our feet,
Echoes of long-forgotten dues,
Resting here through night so sweet.

As dawn peeks through the leafy maze,
Myths entwine with morning light,
Holding fast through fleeting days,
Veils of magic, pure delight.

Threads of Enchantment in the Breeze

Thread by thread, the fabric weaves,
Stitching dreams with gossamer ties,
Caught between the sighing leaves,
Where every whisper softly flies.

Morning breaks with gleaming rays,
Colors dance, a vivid spree,
Nature calls in playful ways,
Entwined with sighs of mystery.

Stories linger in the air,
Floating gently, soft and slow,
Casting spells beyond compare,
In the realm where dreams can grow.

With every breeze, a promise made,
The threads of magic weaving tight,
In the warmth that never fades,
Bringing forth the heart's delight.

Little wonders, bright and bold,
Whisper secrets, urge us near,
In their arms, the world unfolds,
Threads of love that we hold dear.

Tales Spun from Ethereal Threads

In the loom where silence spins,
Tales emerge from woven dreams,
Wanderers and ages blend,
Bound by hope and silver beams.

With each strand, a vision grows,
Winding through the depths of night,
Where the river softly flows,
Casting shadows in the light.

Voices echo on the wind,
Calling out to hearts that roam,
Every story intertwined,
In the heart, they find their home.

Starlit paths and candle glow,
Guide the seekers from afar,
Every journey, tale bestow,
Swimming through the night's own star.

As the dawn begins to break,
Woven threads in sunlight beam,
Shimmering with every ache,
Tell the world of endless dreams.

Whispers Among the Gossamer Leaves

In a glade where whispers play,
Softly dance the leaves so gay.
Moonlight weaves a silver thread,
Among the dreams where magic's spread.

Fingers of the night entwine,
With secrets lost in fragrant pine.
Echoes of a time long past,
In every rustle, shadows cast.

Petals shimmer, dew drops gleam,
Dancing like a fleeting dream.
Listen close, hear nature's sigh,
As stars awaken in the sky.

Gossamer threads in breezes sigh,
Beneath the vast and endless sky.
Each leaf holds tales of joy and woe,
In the quiet night, they gently flow.

So linger here, where whispers weave,
A tapestry that won't deceive.
For in the heart of this embrace,
Magic lives in every space.

Secrets of the Enchanted Grove

Deep within the ancient wood,
Where sunlight filters through the bud.
Magic spills like golden ink,
In every shadow, dreams we think.

Whispers linger in the air,
Carried softly without a care.
Roots entwined with tales untold,
Of knights and fairies bold and old.

Mossy carpets cradle feet,
As secrets stir, the past we meet.
Brambles hold the stories tight,
Guardians of the twilight light.

Breeze that rustles through the oaks,
Shares the laughter, sings the jokes.
In the grove where magic flows,
Heartfelt wonder gently grows.

So wander forth, with open heart,
In every shadow, play your part.
For in this grove, time stops and sways,
A living maze of bygone days.

Silken Shadows at Dusk

As day retreats with gentle grace,
Silk-like shadows start to trace.
Whispers curl like smoke on air,
Filling dusk with tales laid bare.

Crickets chirp a soft refrain,
Beneath the moon, the night's domain.
Stars like diamonds twinkle bright,
In the embrace of tender night.

The world transforms in muted hues,
A canvas painted with deep blues.
Listen close as night unfolds,
In its arms, the magic holds.

Silken threads of twilight dreams,
Weave through soft, ethereal beams.
Secrets lie beneath the boughs,
Waiting for the heart that vows.

So let the shadows wrap you tight,
In dusk's tender, haunting light.
For here among the quiet trees,
Time dances gently on the breeze.

The Lattice of Twilight Tales

In twilight's hush, where stories blend,
A lattice forms, a tale to send.
Each woven thread a memory,
A hint of fate's sweet mystery.

Underneath the eaves of night,
Whispers rise, a gentle flight.
Fables of the brave and true,
Across the sky, they drift anew.

Shadows flicker, soft and shy,
As constellations twinkle high.
Every sighing breath a word,
In this realm where dreams are stirred.

Through the lattice, charms unfold,
In every tale, magic holds.
A tapestry of stars above,
Knit with threads of hope and love.

So enter here, embrace the glow,
Let twilight's tales within you flow.
For in this realm of night's embrace,
You'll find your heart, a sacred place.

The Cloth of Celestial Whispers

In twilight's hush, the stars align,
A tapestry of dreams divine,
Threads of silver, woven bright,
In whispers soft, they kiss the night.

Beneath the moon's celestial gaze,
The shadows dance in mystic ways,
A gentle breeze, the trees reply,
As secrets float like clouds on high.

The nightingale sings of olden lore,
Of heroes' hearts and battles' roar,
In melodies that time won't bind,
Each note a jewel for thee to find.

With every breath, the magic stirs,
Around the world, in silent blurs,
As dreams unfurl on midnight's thread,
A path to realms where few have tread.

So, close your eyes and seek the spark,
In lively tales that you embark,
For in each whisper, echoes dwell,
The cloth of dreams, a mystic spell.

Glimmers Through the Woodland Veil

In forest deep where shadows play,
Glimmers burst through leaf and spray,
A laughter shared by sprite and tree,
In nature's heart, wild and free.

The dappled light, a painter's dream,
Weaves golden threads in twilight's gleam,
Each ray a promise, soft and true,
As secrets bloom on morning dew.

With every step on moss-clad floor,
The whispers call from ancient lore,
Of woodland beings, shy and small,
Who twirl and leap at nature's call.

Through tangled roots and winding trails,
The magic lingers, it never fails,
To twine around the heart so near,
And fill the mind with joy and cheer.

So tread the paths where fairies dwell,
In emerald realms, a living spell,
For in this wood, where glimmers play,
Your spirit dances, lost in sway.

Murmurs Beneath the Starlit Canopy

Beneath the sky, where cosmos sighs,
The nighttime weaves a veil so wise,
It hums a tune of silent dreams,
In twilight's arms, the magic seems.

In every breath, the cosmos speaks,
Of ancient worlds, and starlight peaks,
A gentle pull on heartstrings tight,
As wishes flutter, taking flight.

With silver beams and shadows cast,
The moments linger, fleeting fast,
Each glance reveals a spark of fate,
While whispers weave through twilight's gate.

So softly now, let silence reign,
In starlit warmth, forget your pain,
For under skies, in dreams we meet,
A sanctuary, pure and sweet.

Embrace the night, let worries cease,
In cosmic calm, you'll find your peace,
For in this world of starry gleam,
Each murmur holds a secret dream.

Fables of the Forgotten Glade

In ancient woods where shadows loom,
The glade remembers tales of gloom,
Of lovers lost and battles fought,
In whispered winds, their stories sought.

Amongst the brambles, secrets dwell,
In every mossy stone, a knell,
The sprites recount the fabled past,
In echoes soft, their voices cast.

With every rustle, stories flow,
Of magic kissed by morning's glow,
The trees bend low, their branches sway,
In reverence for the tales that play.

So listen close to nature's heart,
In whispered tones, the voices start,
To weave a fable, rich, profound,
Of love and loss in silence found.

For in this glade, what once has been,
In twilight's light, will always glean,
A timeless bond when day must fade,
In fables held in the forgotten glade.

Echoes of the Enchanted Bough

Beneath the ancient, whispering trees,
Lies a world of forgotten dreams,
Each bough holds secrets in the breeze,
Where silence sings and magic gleams.

In shadows cast by emerald light,
The air is thick with mystery,
Where timid hearts take fearless flight,
Embracing woven history.

With every rustle, stories weave,
Of heroes lost and legends found,
In every sigh, the heart believes,
In echoes rich, the world resounds.

The brook babbles of long-lost days,
As fireflies dance in twilight's glow,
A symphony of gentle ways,
In this enchanted realm we know.

Beneath the moon's soft, silver hue,
Whispers of fate entwine with night,
In every heart, a tale rings true,
To dream in dreams of pure delight.

Threads of Time Tied with Magic

In a loom where shadows play,
The threads of time dance, intertwine,
Each strand a moment, night or day,
Woven with whispers, soft and fine.

With every tug, a memory sparks,
A flicker of laughter lost in air,
The tapestry tells of flickering arcs,
Of bonds created, treasures rare.

Beneath the stars, the fibers glow,
Each hue a tale, a life once spent,
In the weaver's heart, they gently flow,
A song of wonder, time's lament.

A tapestry that knows no bounds,
As colors blend with grace divine,
In every corner, magic sounds,
The rhythm of existence, our lifeline.

So let us spin on destiny's wheel,
And thread our dreams through endless night,
For in each weave, we surely feel,
The touch of fate, the spark of light.

Aria of the Glimmering Grove

Within the grove where shadows play,
The leaves sing soft, a dulcet tune,
A melody that lights the way,
By silver stars and gentle moon.

Each morning's dawn brings dreams anew,
As sunlight filters through the green,
A symphony of life so true,
With every note, the world is seen.

The flowers sway in rhythmic dance,
Their fragrance sweet, a lover's sigh,
In every petal, hope's romance,
To weave a spell beneath the sky.

A brook hums low, its laughter bright,
Reflecting in the shimmering dew,
With every ripple, pure delight,
In harmony, the grove rings true.

As twilight falls, the song persists,
In echoing sighs of dusk's embrace,
For in this grove, where dreams exist,
The heart will find its sacred place.

The Dappled Light of Changing Tales

In dappled light where shadows dance,
Stories tread on whispered breeze,
Each flicker holds a passing chance,
To glimpse the magic in the trees.

With every step, a tale unfolds,
Of creatures brave and journeys grand,
In every heart, a dream that bold,
A legacy across the land.

As leaves turn gold, so do the fates,
With every season, lives entwine,
In cycles vast, the world awaits,
To hear the roots of time align.

The stones remember all that's lost,
And sighs of sprightly youth remain,
For every journey counts the cost,
In the tapestry of joy and pain.

So let the tales be sung aloud,
For in their echoes, we shall find,
A tapestry of joys unbowed,
The changing tales that bind mankind.

Petals and Phantoms in Allegory

In the garden where shadows play,
Petals flutter, bright and gay.
Phantoms whisper secrets old,
As tales of courage gently unfold.

The roses blush with stories rare,
While moonlight dances in the air.
A song unspools in twilight's glow,
Where echoes of the past still flow.

Beneath the boughs, the silence weaves,
A tapestry of dreams and leaves.
In every sigh, a memory gleans,
In every shadow, magic leans.

So wander forth where wonders bloom,
In every petal, dispel the gloom.
For phantoms fade, but truths remain,
In the heart where love's embrace reigns.

Carried on Whispering Winds

Through valleys deep and mountains high,
The winds carry tales that never die.
Whispers of journeys, lost and found,
In rustling leaves, a soft sound.

They speak of dreams on starlit nights,
Of fleeting glories and ancient fights.
On every breeze, a spark ignites,
In each soft sigh, the heart's delights.

From craggy cliffs to meadows wide,
The winds of change become our guide.
With every gust, new paths arise,
In whispered hopes, the soul complies.

So close your eyes, let your heart soar,
Embrace the winds, and seek for more.
For every whisper brings anew,
The promise of a life that's true.

Luminescent Grains of Fantasy

In the midnight hour, starlight spills,
Grains of fantasy dance on hills.
Each glimmer holds a dream untold,
A universe in magic enfolded.

They sparkle bright like the fairest dew,
In the tapestry of night, woven anew.
With every breath, the cosmos sighs,
As imagination takes to the skies.

A wish upon a fleeting star,
Travels through realms both near and far.
In every grain, potential glows,
As tales of whimsy gently flows.

So gather round, let your spirit roam,
In the land where dreamers find their home.
For luminescent grains, oh so slight,
Hold the power to spark pure delight.

The Chronicle of Flickering Lights

In the realm where shadows dwell,
Flickering lights weave a spell.
They dance upon the canvas dark,
Illuminating every lark.

The tales they tell are soft yet bold,
Of heroes' hearts and legends old.
With every glow, a story's spun,
From battles lost to victories won.

Each flicker breathes life to the night,
Chasing away the haunting fright.
In moments caught, dreams take flight,
In the chronicle of sheer delight.

So gather close, let shadows fade,
Embrace the light that memories made.
For every flicker, a future signs,
In the heart where hope aligns.

The Slumbering Wishes of Fablekind

In the hush of the twilight, dreams take flight,
Fablekind whispers secrets, soft and light.
Beneath the moon's gentle, silver gleam,
Every wish entwines within a shared dream.

The stars gather close, their stories unfold,
Once forgotten tales, now brave and bold.
In the heart of the night, they silently vow,
To grant all the wishes, here and now.

With each twinkling glimmer, hope ignites,
We dance on the currents of magical nights.
Fables that linger in shadows and sighs,
Curled up in the folds of the midnight skies.

Awake are the dreams that in slumber reside,
They shimmer like jewels, a cosmic guide.
With petals of stardust, we weave the air,
In the cradle of wish, all hearts lay bare.

So hush now, dear dreamers, let fantasies flow,
For Fablekind's wishes are waiting to grow.
In gardens of night where hope gently sways,
We harvest the magic from slumbering days.

Melodies Within a Glance

In the dim light of evening, sweet notes arise,
Each glance a harmony, under starlit skies.
A whisper of laughter, a flutter of grace,
Melodies linger, time holds its place.

Every heartbeat echoes, a rhythm divine,
Eyes meet with a spark; two souls intertwine.
A glance carries stories, unspoken, profound,
In that fleeting moment, true magic is found.

Soft breezes carry the tunes of the night,
Dance of the shadows, the world feels so right.
With every soft glance, the world spins anew,
In silence we listen, as dreams come to view.

Moments like these, brushed with pure gold,
In the tapestry woven, young hearts are bold.
Though nothing is written, the song finds its way,
Melodies sing to the dawn's gentle sway.

So cherish the echoes that glimmer and shine,
For in every glance, a universe's design.
The heart, like a songbird, will always take flight,
In the cadence of love, through day and through night.

Scent of Jasmine in the Dreamscape

In the depths of the night, a fragrance will flow,
Jasmine whispers secrets only dreamers know.
A soft veil of petals, in twilight they dance,
Cradled in whispers, they weave a romance.

Through shadows of slumber, the blossoms sway,
Each scent tells a tale in a delicate way.
Like memories captured in vaporous trails,
Jasmine's sweet breath in the moonlight prevails.

In gardens of longing, the dreams intertwine,
The stars hold their breath in a shimmering line.
With every soft sigh drifting over the sand,
The fragrance of jasmine beckons our hand.

Lost in a reverie, we twirl and we glide,
In this dreamscape of night, where wonder abides.
The scent of sweet moments, escaping our grasp,
Twines through the air, like the past in a clasp.

So linger a moment, breathe deep, then depart,
Let jasmine embrace you, and mend every heart.
For in every whisper, a treasure we find,
The soft scent of jasmine lingers in mind.

The Mirage of Silken Threads

In the weave of the night, silken threads softly gleam,
A mirage of visions, elusive as dreams.
With colors that flutter, like whispers in flight,
We dance 'neath the tapestry woven of light.

Each slender thread tells of moments untold,
A flicker of memories, both tender and bold.
In shadows we follow, their shimmer and weave,
Unraveling stories that hearts dare conceive.

In the tapestry's depths, where secrets reside,
Threads pull us closer, and time's gentle tide.
Like a soft lullaby, they cradle our fears,
Silken threads of magic, spun from hopes and tears.

With echoes of laughter that float through the air,
The mirage, a promise; a wish we all share.
In the fabric of dreams, we forever belong,
Silken threads of connection, a delicate song.

So let us embrace the enchantment we find,
In the mirage of threads, our souls intertwined.
For in every gesture, a story, a thread,
A journey unending, where dreams are well-fed.

Blossoms of Lore on the Edge of Night

In twilight's embrace, the whispers flow,
Beneath the stars, where secrets grow.
Petals unfurl, soft as a sigh,
In the garden of dreams, where shadows lie.

Ancient tales in the moonlight gleam,
With every bloom, we chase the dream.
A dance of spirits, both bold and shy,
Time weaves its patterns, like a lullaby.

The air hums sweet, with fragments of lore,
In silence, the night holds treasures galore.
As lanterns flicker with a tender light,
We gather the magic, deep in the night.

Nature's symphony sings soft refrain,
Drawing us closer, binding our chain.
Each blossom a story, each leaf a sigh,
In the garden of dusk, where dreams fly high.

So linger a moment, let time dissolve,
In the arms of the night, let our hearts resolve.
For blossoms of lore beckon from sight,
Whispering softly of wonders tonight.

The Flicker of Hidden Glances

In crowded rooms where silence speaks,
A flicker of eyes, the heart's mystique.
An unspoken word hangs in the air,
A glance exchanged, a curious dare.

Between two souls, a spark ignites,
In shadows deep, where warmth invites.
A mirror of thoughts, so close, yet far,
Each fleeting moment, a shimmering star.

Layers unfold with the softest gaze,
In the dance of night, we're lost in a haze.
Whispers of longing carried on sighs,
In the world of secrets, where the heart lies.

The thrill of the chase, the fear of the fall,
In hidden corners, we heed the call.
With every glance, a story to weave,
In the tapestry of time, we dare to believe.

So linger a while in this silent trance,
Embrace the magic of chance and chance.
For hidden glances hold worlds divine,
In the blink of an eye, our spirits entwine.

Dreams Woven with Wands of Time

In the quiet of night, where dreams take flight,
Wands of time weave their magic bright.
Threads of the past intertwine with now,
As we glimpse the wonder, we wonder how.

Each wish a spell, cast in the dark,
With every heartbeat, we leave our mark.
A tapestry spun from whispers and sighs,
In the realm of dreams, where the spirit flies.

Moments unspooled, like ribbons of light,
Twisting and turning, ready for flight.
We float on the currents, enchanted and free,
In the canvas of time, just you and me.

Past, present, future, a delicate blend,
In dreams woven softly, the magic won't end.
With each gentle breeze, a story unfolds,
In the heart of the night, where hope never cold.

So reach for the stars, let your heart be prime,
For dreams are the treasures that dance with time.
In the world of enchantment where echoes roam,
We'll wander together, forever at home.

The Allure of Velvet Secrets

In shadows deep, where secrets nest,
Velvet whispers call to the restless quest.
Soft as a sigh, wrapped in the night,
In the dance of shadows, we seek the light.

Mysterious smiles flicker and sway,
Shrouded in silence, they lead us astray.
Each thread of darkness, a tale to unveil,
In the allure of secrets, we follow the trail.

The heart beats faster, curiosity ignites,
As whispers entwine like moonlit lights.
In the fabric of time, our fates intertwine,
Chasing the echoes of love's design.

With every heartbeat, tensions rise,
As the allure deepens, we lose track of ties.
In corners forgotten, where hopes lay bare,
We dance to the rhythm that hangs in the air.

So linger in twilight, where dreams take form,
In the velvet embrace, be lost in the swarm.
For secrets hold magic, the finest of threads,
In the allure of night, where adventure spreads.

Tales Carved in Elven Wood

In the glades where shadows dance,
Whispers speak of days long gone.
Elven hearts in silence prance,
Beneath the ancient yew and dawn.

Stories entwined in branches high,
With leaves that shimmer, softly sigh,
Each secret told in rustling breeze,
Echoes of time among the trees.

Glorious tales of love and fate,
Carved by hands both gentle, great.
Fables sung in twilight's glow,
Filling the night, with memories slow.

Moonlit pathways softly gleam,
Leading to a world of dreams.
Where shadows hide, and starlight weaves,
The magic of what nature leaves.

In every knot, a story holds,
In every grain, a truth unfolds.
Through elven woods, the wanderers roam,
Each heartbeat whispers, "This is home."

Mysteries Woven in Stardust

Beneath the veil of nebulae bright,
Secrets shimmer through the night.
Cosmic tales of ancient lore,
In every glimmer, so much more.

Stars collide in a dance divine,
Each twinkle holds a fate entwined.
Nebulas cradle dreams unseen,
Vast and endless, flowing green.

Galaxies swim in black velvet seas,
Tales carried on celestial breeze.
A tapestry of wishes cast,
Promises of futures, tethered fast.

Planets spin on their silent paths,
Chasing shadows, evoking laughs.
In the depths of space, mysteries sing,
Of worlds where time is not a thing.

With every comet that streaks away,
Hopes resound in bright array.
We look above, and in awe we trust,
The wonders of life—woven in stardust.

The Lattice of Unsaid Dreams

In twilight's hush, a lattice grows,
Of dreams that linger, yet none knows.
Threads of thought and wishes spun,
A fragile tapestry begun.

Hidden hopes in each whisper blend,
Paths untaken, journeys unbent.
In silence hums the heart's refrain,
A melody of joy and pain.

Each unvoiced wish holds tight its thread,
In shadows where the brave have tread.
Lives entwined in choices made,
The lattice shapes the masquerade.

Fading echoes of laughter bright,
In the quiet depths of night.
A glimpse of what could be, a sigh,
As dreams awake and softly fly.

Beneath the stars, we weave and mend,
Tales of kindness, love to lend.
In this lattice, truth lays gleamed,
The patterns of our unsaid dreams.

Gossamer Threads of Forgotten Lore

In the corner of a dusty book,
Lie whispers of the world we took.
Gossamer threads of tales once spun,
Fading like the setting sun.

Ghostly figures in pages worn,
Of knights and wizards, battles sworn.
Softly beckoning those who seek,
The voices of the past they speak.

Through ivy thick and briars deep,
The secrets of the old ones keep.
A tapestry of ancient days,
In sunlight's glow, a gentle haze.

Heartfelt dreams, forever chased,
In each line, memories graced.
Stories lost in time's embrace,
Yearning still for a warm embrace.

With each turn of fateful page,
Lives anew in every age.
To chase those threads, let hearts implore,
The gossamer weave of forgotten lore.

Elfin Echoes in the Emerald Vale

In emerald glades, where whispering winds,
Dance between trees where soft light begins.
Elves sing sweet songs, as shadows take flight,
In harmony woven, both day and the night.

Moss carpets paths where the ancients tread,
With tales of the forest, so wondrously spread.
Each leaf tells a story of time long ago,
In the chorus of life, where magic will flow.

Beneath silken boughs, where moonlight does stream,
The echoes of laughter blend with a dream.
A flicker of starlight doth guide every roam,
In the heart of the vale, where elves call their home.

Glimmers of laughter, like dew on the grass,
In a world of enchantment, the moments will pass.
With every soft footstep, a bond will ignite,
In the elfin embrace, all shadows take flight.

So linger a while, let your spirit take wing,
In this emerald vale, where the elves softly sing.
With hearts intertwined, in the song of the night,
Let the magic of friendship forever take flight.

Secrets Carved by Starlight

In the stillness of night, when the world holds its breath,
Stars carve their stories of life and of death.
Each shimmer a whisper from far, far away,
Tales of forgotten, where shadows will play.

A tapestry woven in glimmers of light,
Unveils ancient secrets, shrouded from sight.
As comet tails dance and the moon casts her glow,
The starlit unfurling of truths we may know.

Beneath velvet skies, where wishes take form,
The heartbeats of dreams rise and fall with the storm.
Hushed voices echo through timeless expanse,
Inviting the curious to join in the dance.

With wishes like lanterns, we cast them on high,
To shimmer and spark in the deep ink-black sky.
The mysteries whispered in twilight's soft hand,
Awaken our spirits to wonders unplanned.

So gather your hopes, under starlit embrace,
In the quiet of night, find your rightful place.
For secrets are waiting, just listen, be true,
In this cosmic ballet, they're waiting for you.

Shadows Dancing in the Wisp of Dawn

As twilight surrenders to dawn's gentle kiss,
Shadows emerge from the depths of the mist.
They sway in the light with a flickering grace,
In the moment of stillness, find your own place.

With whispers of promise that bid night goodbye,
The world stirs awake, as the sun starts to rise.
In hues of soft orange and tinges of gold,
New stories awaken, like secrets retold.

Jewel-bright dewdrops on petals will gleam,
As shadows, they twirl in the first light of dream.
The dance of the dawn is a magical sight,
Where the veil thins gently, between dark and light.

So let every heartbeat find rhythm anew,
In the dance of the dawn, let your spirit break through.
The shadows, they beckon, as day calls your name,
In the wisp of the dawn, find the spark in the flame.

For in every motion, in each fleeting glance,
Lives the heartbeat of life, in an endless romance.
In the shadows that mingle with morning's soft sigh,
Are the dreams yet to awaken, beneath the wide sky.

Glistening Secrets of the Hearth

In the warmth of the hearth, where the embers glow
bright,
Gathered tales swirl in the soft, flick'rous light.
The secrets of old whisper softly to me,
In the flicker of flames, they long to be free.

With each crackle echoing memories dear,
A symphony rises, inviting us near.
The scent of the spices, a homey embrace,
Where laughter and stories forever find space.

Glistening candles with shadows that twine,
Craft a tapestry rich where the heart defines.
In this circle of comfort, all worries are shed,
As time gently pauses, our spirits are fed.

So, sit by the fire, let the night gently weave,
Moments of magic for those who believe.
In the glimmering glow, let the stories be heard,
For in shared tales of life, destiny's blurred.

This hearth, it will cradle the dreams and the sighs,
As embers will spark with the glow of our ties.
In the lingering warmth, discover the art,
Of glistening secrets that dwell in the heart.

Petals of Desire in Gossamer Threads

In gardens where the whispers bloom,
Petals dance with sweet perfume.
Threads of silver, soft and bright,
Weave the dreams that kiss the night.

A shimmering light in twilight's grace,
Caught in the heart, a sacred place.
Each sigh of wind, a longing song,
In nature's grasp, we all belong.

Where shadows play with gentle hues,
And time drips slow as evening blues.
Desires flutter, softly spun,
Underneath the setting sun.

In every bloom, a tale untold,
Of love that dares to be so bold.
With gossamer threads that entwine,
Hearts embrace what's pure, divine.

So let us wander, hand in hand,
In this enchanted, dream-filled land.
For petals fall like whispered prayers,
In silence shared, in lovers' lairs.

Timeless Echoes of Magic's Breath

In whispered woods where shadows play,
Magic lingers, night and day.
Timeless echoes, soft and keen,
Speak of places yet unseen.

With every heartbeat, spells take flight,
Carried on the wings of night.
From ancient trees, the stories weave,
In each, a promise, none believe.

The moonlit path, a guiding script,
Where secrets dwell, and faeries slip.
In corners dark, the magic brews,
A dance of old, with vibrant hues.

Each breath, a chance to cast the past,
In moments brief, enchantments last.
With every wish, a star descends,
Connecting hearts, where magic bends.

So close your eyes and feel the change,
As time unwinds, a wondrous range.
In echoes soft, our spirits soar,
Through portals wide, forever more.

Vows Held by Starlit Ferns

In hidden groves where starlight shimmers,
Vows entwined like whispered glimmers.
By ferns aglow in silver light,
Hearts find solace in the night.

Promises made in shadows cast,
In twilight's grasp, forever last.
With every leaf, a secret shared,
In tender moments, love declared.

Each sigh of wind, a sacred chant,
In nature's arms, our spirits dance.
With every twirl, the magic swells,
In starlit realms where silence dwells.

Let us gather where dreams ignite,
Underneath the pale moonlight.
For vows held close, like fern leaves sway,
Bind our souls 'til break of day.

So linger here, in shadows deep,
In promises that never sleep.
For in this grove, beneath the sky,
Our love, like ferns, will never die.

Beneath the Canopy of Soft Sighs

In glades adorned with gentle lays,
We drift beneath the sun's warm rays.
A canopy of whispers sighs,
Where dreams are spun in soft replies.

The brook's sweet song, a lullaby,
Wraps us close, as time drifts by.
With every step, the earth shall bend,
In nature's dance, our hearts transcend.

Each leafy branch a witness stands,
To whispered thoughts and holding hands.
In every rustle, secrets shared,
In silent vows, we're gently bared.

So let us wander, lost in grace,
In shadows deep, we find our place.
For underneath the boughs so high,
Love's echo breathes, a tender sigh.

As twilight wraps in velvet hue,
We cherish moments, pure and true.
Beneath the stars, we'll find our way,
In the magic of the fading day.

Phantoms of Enchantment in the Glen

In whispers low, the phantoms play,
Among the trees where echoes stay.
A glimmer here, a shadow there,
They dance with grace, a ghostly air.

Beneath the moon, they weave their tale,
In silver light, where dreams unveil.
With laughter soft, like distant chimes,
In glen of magic, lost in rhymes.

Each footstep stirs the ancient ground,
In hidden paths where dreams abound.
They speak of secrets, old as time,
In every murmur, every rhyme.

With flowing robes and eyes aglow,
They beckon forth, to follow slow.
Through twinkling stars and misty lace,
They guide the heart to a hidden place.

So heed the call, if you should dare,
For phantoms dance in twilight air.
In enchanted glen, where night is spun,
The magic waits for everyone.

Veil of Secrets in the Faery Light

Beneath the stars, where shadows creep,
A veil of secrets, soft and deep.
In faery light, the stories twine,
Between the worlds, where spirits shine.

A lantern glow, a flick'ring spark,
In hidden nooks, where whispers hark.
The fae unfold their tales of yore,
Of ancient lore and legends core.

With laughter bright, they twirl and sway,
In circles spun where dreams convey.
Each twinkle speaks of hopes pursued,
In faery lands, where hearts are wooed.

Through mossy banks and dappled glade,
A tapestry of night is laid.
In every sigh, a secret told,
In faery light, both warm and cold.

So seek the veil, the mystic thread,
Where dreams ignite and spirits wed.
In timeless night, let worries fade,
And dance with faeries in the glade.

Dance of Shadows on Sylvan Strings

In twilight's grasp, the shadows sway,
On sylvan strings, they weave their play.
A tapestry of night unfurls,
As magic breathes through dreaming whirls.

With whispered notes, the forest hums,
While playful shadows softly come.
They leap and twirl, a waltz so light,
In dances spun with pure delight.

The trees, they sway with rhythm sweet,
As shadows whirl 'round nimble feet.
In melodies of dusk, they soar,
Where echoes linger, evermore.

Each flicker bright, a starry beam,
In this enchanted, moonlit dream.
The night their stage, the stars their key,
As shadows dance in harmony.

So let your heart take flight tonight,
With shadows twirling in the light.
In sylvan dreams, the magic sings,
In every pause, sweet evening clings.

Charms Hidden in the Misty Glade

Where whispers curl in foggy guise,
In misty glade, the magic lies.
With every step, a charm unfolds,
In nature's heart, where life beholds.

The air is thick with olden spells,
In dew-kissed leaves, where fortune dwells.
Each glimmer hints at tales untold,
In hidden paths, where dreams are bold.

Among the ferns, a secret song,
A melody that sweeps along.
It calls the heart to seek the true,
In misty glades, where wonders grew.

Through bramble thick and shadows deep,
The charm of night wraps dreams in sleep.
With every sigh, a hope reborn,
In nature's magic, new and worn.

So linger here, where spirits glide,
In misty glade, let dreams abide.
For charms are woven in the air,
In whispers soft, both light and rare.

Murmurs from the Twilight Knoll

In shadows deep where whispers creep,
The twilight knoll holds dreams to keep.
A crescent moon, a silver thread,
Weaves tales of stars, where night is led.

The breeze hums low, a secret song,
Of fleeting moments, where we belong.
A dance of leaves with gentle grace,
In twilight's arms, we find our place.

The fireflies flicker, a lantern's glow,
In the heart of dusk, their magic flows.
With every flutter, they trace the air,
As if they carry a whispered prayer.

The world holds still, as time takes pause,
In nature's rhythm, we find the cause.
The knoll, a keeper of secrets held,
Where wishes bloom, and dreams are spelled.

Fables on the Edge of Reality

In shadows cast by the setting sun,
Where fables whisper, and stories run.
A realm between the seen and unseen,
Awaits the hearts that dare to dream.

A tapestry spun with threads of gold,
Each tale a treasure, waiting to unfold.
In echoes soft, the voices call,
To daring souls, who risk it all.

The midnight owl hoots a warning clear,
Of realms that shimmer, both far and near.
A bridge of thoughts, a leap of faith,
To cross the line where dreams create.

In every fable, a lesson sown,
A map to follow, a path unknown.
For truth and myth, forever twine,
In the dance of life, pure and divine.

So heed the stories, let them inspire,
For on their edge, we learn to fly higher.
With each brave step, the world expands,
And our hearts bloom wide, like open hands.

The Alchemy of Thistle and Time

In fields where thistles bend and sway,
Lies an alchemy of night and day.
With roots that grasp the soil so tight,
They whisper secrets to the light.

Time flows slowly like the river's bend,
Where every moment's both foe and friend.
In thistle's bloom, the wisdom hums,
Of journeys waited, and promise comes.

Amidst the thorns, the beauty grows,
In bristled strength, the heart knows.
Each petal holds a tale untold,
Of courage found and fears controlled.

The seasons dance to nature's rhyme,
As time unfolds its precious prime.
In thistle's grasp, the stories blend,
A magic forged that will not end.

So cherish the moments, calm and chime,
For life's true treasure is in the time.
With every thistle, let love unwind,
In the alchemy of heart and mind.

Phantoms in the Dew-Kissed Dawn

At dawn's first breath, a silence reigns,
Where phantoms linger, free from chains.
With dew-kissed grass, the world awakes,
To whispered dreams and gentle shakes.

The golden light spills o'er the hills,
As memories dance like autumn chills.
In every glimmer, stories stir,
Of bygone days and how they blur.

The echoes of laughter, soft and sweet,
Resound in places where shadows meet.
With every step, the past draws near,
In fleeting glimpses, held so dear.

The breeze carries secrets, old yet new,
In the warm embrace of morning dew.
For in the dawn, we learn to see,
The beauty in what used to be.

So rise with the sun, and dare to dream,
For phantoms bear tales that brightly gleam.
In each new light, let spirits roam,
And find your heart in the day's soft home.

Whispers Beneath the Canopy

In the depths where the willow sighs,
Whispers dance on the evening breeze,
Words carried on wings of fireflies,
Secrets held in the rustling leaves.

Glimmers of dawn through branches weave,
Tales of magic in emerald hues,
Where shadows play and hearts believe,
In the twilight's enchanting muse.

Underneath, where the shadows prance,
Stories linger like a forgotten dream,
Every rustle a fleeting chance,
To feel the pulse of a hidden theme.

The canopy breathes with a heart so old,
The whispers soft as a lover's vow,
Under the guidance of starlight bold,
The forest hums a solemn bow.

Through the night, the magic sways,
With every sigh, the world transforms,
In the embrace of the moonlit rays,
Whispers tell of the age-old norms.

Secrets Spun from Moonlight

Beneath the gaze of the watchful moon,
Secrets weave like silken threads,
Strands of silver in a timeless tune,
Where the night spills what daylight dreads.

Gentle echoes waltz on the air,
Whispered wishes in the tranquil glow,
Each untouched moment holds a prayer,
As the quiet realm begins to grow.

Shadows dance to the rhythm of night,
Beneath the trees whose roots entwine,
Hidden realms shimmer, soft and bright,
In the tapestry of a design divine.

Secrets nestled in the cool, soft earth,
Carried forth by the playful breeze,
Each starlit story sparks rebirth,
Where silence bows and the heart finds ease.

As dawn creeps in, the magic fades,
But the whispers linger, soft and shy,
In every color the sunlight trades,
The moonlight's secrets will never die.

Echoes of Enchantment and Sorrow

In the forest deep where shadows dwell,
Echoes weave a tale of the night,
Enchanted whispers, a wishing well,
A bittersweet song of lost delight.

Each breath of wind a memory shared,
With leaves that twirl in a gentle sway,
Holding close what the heart has dared,
To safeguard dreams that fade away.

Starlit paths where old souls roam,
Glimmering hearts find solace there,
Between the worlds both strange and home,
In the silence, love's shadow glare.

The ravens cry as the twilight passes,
Mournful notes in the evening air,
In the glade where time sassily glasses,
Enchantments linger, gliding with care.

Yet in the sorrow, beauty thrives,
Every echo a breath of grace,
For the heart that loves forever strives,
In echoes that time cannot erase.

Shadows of the Glimmering Grove

In the grove where the shadows play,
Glimmers wink like stars above,
Every corner holds night and day,
Cradled softly in endless love.

Moonbeams dance on the dew-kissed grass,
A melody woven from dreams and light,
With every step, tales start to amass,
As shadows twirl in the soft twilight.

Ancient trees with their stories bare,
Guarding secrets of earth and sky,
With every rustle, a whispered prayer,
For shadows that watch and keep nearby.

The air thickens with a lingering charm,
As the world slows in the quiet glow,
Wrapped in magic, safe from harm,
In the embrace of the glimmering show.

Where shadows meet and magic flows,
In the heart of the grove, an eternal trance,
Every heartbeat in the twilight grows,
A dance of shadows, a timeless romance.

Whims of the Hidden Glimmer

In the woods where shadows play,
Tiny lights dance and sway,
Whispers carried on the breeze,
Secrets hidden in the trees.

Moonlit paths of silver hue,
Magic stirs in every view,
Glimmers shine through tangled vines,
Nature's secrets intertwine.

Gentle laughter, soft and light,
Echoes fade as day turns night,
Cascading stars above the stream,
The forest holds a whispered dream.

Step by step, the heart shall find,
Truths that linger, souls entwined,
Fragrant petals in the air,
A world of wonder, bright and rare.

So let the whimsy guide your feet,
Where the hidden glimmers meet,
Embrace the magic, take your chance,
In the forest's mystic dance.

Nectar of the Nightingale's Lore

Under starlight, soft and low,
Nightingales sing tales we know,
Harmonies of ancient lore,
Echoing from a secret shore.

With each note, the shadows flee,
Dancing light, a tapestry,
Tales of love and trials bold,
In their song, the past unfolds.

From the depths of tangled thorns,
Rise the stories, new and worn,
A nectar sweet, a dreamer's flight,
Carried on the wings of night.

In the hush, a promise made,
Whispers shared in twilight's shade,
Hope ignites like dawn's first glow,
While nightingales weave joy below.

So linger long, let echoes weave,
In the magic we believe,
For in the song, the heart will soar,
To taste the nectar evermore.

Enchanted Secrets in the Thicket

In the thicket, shadows weave,
Mysteries that hearts conceive,
Hidden paths that twist and turn,
Where the lanterns softly burn.

Leaves a-shimmer with delight,
Guard the secrets of the night,
Dappled moonlight on the ground,
Whispers soft, a gentle sound.

From the depths where fairies glint,
Magic breathes in every tint,
Woven dreams in silken threads,
Stories linger where hope spreads.

Hear the rustle, feel the breeze,
Every heartbeat, every tease,
Nature's magic, wild and free,
Where enchanted spirits be.

So venture forth, the heart embraced,
In the thicket, joy is traced,
Secrets linger, waiting tight,
In the shadows, dance with light.

Whirlwind of Silvery Secrets

In a whirl of silvery light,
Mysteries twirl into the night,
Swirling breezes through the trees,
Carrying whispers on the breeze.

Stars above begin to gleam,
Softly lighting every dream,
In the canvas of the sky,
Secrets hidden, drifting by.

Caught in laughter's sweet embrace,
Every moment leaves a trace,
Glints of silver in the air,
Magic blooms from everywhere.

Beneath the moon's watchful eye,
Time seems endless, like a sigh,
Journey on through night's delight,
In the whirlwind, hearts take flight.

So catch a glimmer, hold it near,
In the silence, truths appear,
Let the whirlwind spin you round,
In its magic, joy is found.

The Curation of Celestial Hues

In twilight's brush, the colors glow,
A tapestry of dreams in flow.
Amidst the stars, they softly blend,
A myriad of journeys, they transcend.

Whispers of azure and gold combine,
Each hue a story, each shade divine.
The cosmos holds its vibrant art,
A dance of wonders, a beating heart.

From indigo nights to amber dawns,
The palette sings, and silence fawns.
Celestial wonders sway and twine,
In gentle whispers, fate aligns.

With every glance, a soul takes flight,
Through chromatic paths of endless night.
In cosmic realms, the heart can see,
The curation of what's meant to be.

With tender grace, the heavens weave,
A shelter where all hearts believe.
In every hue, a promise lies,
The universe sings beneath our skies.

Fleeting Footsteps on Mossy Stones

Along the brook, soft footsteps tread,
Where mossy stones cradle dreams unsaid.
Each echo holds a fleeting breath,
A dance with time, a whispering death.

The forest hums a gentle song,
While shadows play and spirits throng.
In every step, a tale is spun,
Of ancient paths and battles won.

Through silver leaves, the sunlight streams,
Awakening lost and tangled dreams.
Each stone remembers the touch of fate,
In the quiet woods, we contemplate.

Yet as we walk, the moment fades,
Like autumn leaves that softly cascade.
In memories etched upon the breeze,
We find our hearts, we find our peace.

So linger not; let footprints shine,
On mossy stones where our souls entwine.
For fleeting are the hours we share,
In nature's arms, with love laid bare.

Dusty Tomes of the Otherworld

In shadows deep, where secrets sleep,
Dusty tomes their riddles keep.
Bound and worn, each page a sigh,
Of whispered tales that never die.

Through ink and parchment, voices call,
Entreating those who dare to sprawl.
In forgotten corners, wisdom waits,
Unlocking pathways, opening gates.

Ghostly echoes from ages past,
In every line, a spell is cast.
With stories woven in mystic night,
These dusty tomes unveil the light.

By candle's glow, the past ignites,
Each verse a dream through endless nights.
In every chapter, the truth resides,
As lost souls wander, the page divides.

So take a breath and turn a page,
Join the dance of the timeless sage.
In dusty tomes, our fate aligns,
Where every word forever shines.

Songs of the Glade's Guardians

In emerald depths where secrets bloom,
The guardians sing to dispel the gloom.
With voices sweet as the morning dew,
They weave enchantments, both old and new.

Beneath the canopy where shadows play,
The melodies of twilight sway.
Each note a thread in nature's loom,
Binding all hearts, dispelling doom.

With every flutter of leaf and wing,
The glade awakens, and echoes ring.
They dance in circles, wild and free,
Awakening spirits, a symphony.

From ancient oaks to silver streams,
The songs are laced with gentle dreams.
Through twilight's veil, the magic flows,
As harmony in the stillness grows.

So listen close, and heed their call,
For in their songs, we find our all.
In the glade's embrace, our souls align,
With guardians' music, forever divine.

Folklore Woven with Silver Linings

In the heart of whispers twine,
Fables gleam like silver wine.
Echoes of the ancients call,
A tapestry where shadows fall.

Moonlit paths and starlit dreams,
Dance within the silver seams.
Legends breathe on twilight shores,
Guarded by the ancient lore.

Beneath the boughs of elder trees,
Secrets rustle in the breeze.
Each tale a star in night's embrace,
Shimmering with time and grace.

Glimmers of the past reside,
Within the folds of heart's deep tide.
Bound in love's eternal clutch,
We hear the stories, feel the touch.

Woven threads of fate divine,
Knit together, yours and mine.
In the woods where shadows play,
Folklore sings at close of day.

Chimeras of Celestial Delights

Up above, the night unfurls,
Dreams are stitched in starry swirls.
Whispers of the cosmos glow,
Chimeras dance, both fast and slow.

Fairy tales in astral hue,
Glide through skies of velvet blue.
In the realm of twinkling sights,
Wonders hum of endless nights.

Nebulas in splendor play,
Painting hopes beneath the gray.
Guided by the spark of light,
Spirits soar to take their flight.

Each celestial twist, a song,
Telling tales of right and wrong.
Specters of the dreams we chase,
In the vast, enchanting space.

Golden threads of fate entwine,
In the dark, our hearts align.
Chimeras whisper soft and low,
Painting worlds where wishes flow.

Resonance of Secrets Underneath the Stars

Beneath the quilt of night's embrace,
Secrets linger, veiled in grace.
Sighs of silence hum through trees,
In the cool and gentle breeze.

Each twinkle holds a story deep,
Awakening those lost in sleep.
Moonbeams weave with mystic art,
Binding light to every heart.

In the stillness, echoes share,
Whispers of a world laid bare.
Resonance of dreams in flight,
Stirring shadows, birthing light.

Every heartbeat, a secret told,
In silver tones and threads of gold.
Beneath the stars, we find our way,
Guided by the night's soft play.

From cryptic runes of ages past,
Glories flicker, free and vast.
In this realm, we dare to roam,
For in the dark, we find our home.

Tracks of the Elfin Flare

In twilight's glow, the trails appear,
Footprints light with laughter clear.
Elfin whispers, soft and sly,
Drawn by lights that cloak the sky.

Glimmers dance on forest floors,
Mapping paths to ancient shores.
Every flicker holds the key,
Unlocking realms of fantasy.

Wanders of the mystic kind,
Set to nature's gentle bind.
Following the sparkling trail,
Guided by the elfin gale.

Moonbeams waltz on winding streams,
Pouring life into our dreams.
Tracks alive with magic rare,
Filling hearts with elfin flare.

As day surrenders softly now,
To night's embrace and silent vow.
We wander where the starlight beams,
Chasing echoes of our dreams.

Beneath the Glinting Faerie Veil

In shadows deep where whispers dwell,
The faeries weave their timeless spell.
With glinting eyes and laughter bright,
They dance beneath the silver light.

In glades adorned with sapphire blooms,
They twirl and spin, dispelling glooms.
A tapestry of dreams unfurled,
In secret realms of magic swirled.

Their wings, like gossamer threads of dawn,
Embrace the night when day is gone.
And in the hush, a song takes flight,
Beneath the glinting faerie light.

The stars above begin to gleam,
As faerie hearts ignite the dream.
In every sigh, a wish is made,
In every dance, a promise laid.

So wander forth, O brave and bold,
In tales of wonder yet untold.
For those who seek and dare to tread,
May find the dreams that softly spread.

The Archive of Lost Wishes

In an attic dim, where time stands still,
The whispers echo, soft and shrill.
An archive lies of heartfelt dreams,
Where yearning fades and silence beams.

With dust-streaked tomes and pages worn,
Each wish was crafted, gently sworn.
In candlelight, the secrets glow,
Of lives once lived, of paths not shown.

The fluttering pages beckon near,
Each sigh of hope, a tale sincere.
Some wishes rusted, others bright,
Awaiting hearts to reignite.

But wishes lost may find their way,
In twilight's arms at end of day.
For every dream that fades from sight,
Is held in shadows, wrapped in light.

So grasp the threads of what once was,
And weave your fate with gentle cause.
For in the archive, still they wait,
The lost wishes that shape our fate.

Pollen and Petals: An Ancient Chorus

In gardens lush where petals sway,
The ancient chorus finds its way.
With pollen dust and fragrant air,
Each bloom rejoices in its care.

The daisies chatter in delight,
While roses blush in soft moonlight.
Their voices rise in harmony,
A symphony of memory.

The bees partake in buzzing song,
While nature sings where hearts belong.
Through whispers sweet, the flowers share,
A tale of love that lingers there.

In sunlit beams, the petals dance,
In every breeze, a fleeting chance.
To feel the pulse of earth's embrace,
To weave through time in nature's grace.

So tread the paths where blossoms dwell,
And listen close; the stories tell.
With pollen and petal as guides,
The ancient chorus ever abides.

Dances of the Sylvan Spirits

In wooded realms where moonlight bends,
The sylvan spirits weave amends.
With laughter soft and twinkling eyes,
They paint the night with whispered sighs.

Beneath the boughs, their shadows play,
In twilight's arms, they gently sway.
With every rustle, every glance,
They beckon forth a secret dance.

The leaves respond to ancient songs,
As nature hums where magic throngs.
Each moment spins in graceful flight,
As spirits dance through starry night.

The owls call out in solemn tune,
While fireflies waltz beneath the moon.
Their gleeful steps, a fleeting trace,
Of joy entwined in woodland space.

So venture forth to where they gleam,
Embrace the magic, touch the dream.
In dances wild, let spirits roam,
For in the woods, we all are home.

The Sigh of Twilight's Mirage

In twilight's embrace, shadows blend,
A dance of whispers, where colors bend.
The moon hangs low, a silver grace,
A fleeting sigh in this timeless space.

As stars awaken, secrets unfurl,
Each twinkle a promise, a shimmering pearl.
The night's gentle breath stirs the trees,
A lullaby wrapped in a soft, cool breeze.

In the hush of dusk, dreams take flight,
Guided by fireflies, glowing bright.
They carry wishes on gossamer wings,
To realms unseen, where magic sings.

The horizon blushes, a canvas anew,
With strokes of plum and a hint of blue.
A sigh escapes as day meets night,
In this twilight mirage, pure delight.

So linger awhile, let your heart sway,
In twilight's embrace, where shadows play.
For in this hour, dreams interlace,
A tapestry woven in ethereal grace.

Lullabies of the Hidden Realm

Beneath the willow, secrets lie,
Where whispered lore catches the eye.
Lullabies drift on the gentle air,
In the hidden realm, beyond despair.

The brook hums softly, a timeless tune,
Kissed by the light of the silver moon.
Each stone a keeper of tales long past,
In echoes of laughter, memories cast.

Flickering fireflies dance and glide,
Through a world where shadows reside.
Each glimmer a spark of wonder bright,
Guiding the lost through the quiet night.

Time bows down in this secret nest,
Entranced by the moments so tenderly blessed.
Each sigh and murmur, a woven spell,
In the hidden realm where spirits dwell.

So come, dear friend, lay your worries low,
In lullabies soft, let your spirit flow.
For in this haven, solace is found,
In the hidden realm, where dreams abound.

Whispers of Petals' Dream

In gardens where petals weave their song,
Each blossom whispers of tales so long.
The fragrance twirls on the soft spring air,
A dream unfolding, delicate and rare.

Among the daisies, secrets entwine,
In the hush of dawn, where sunbeams shine.
Butterflies flutter, their colors bold,
Carving the essence of stories told.

The roses blush, a gentle sigh,
While daisies giggle and drift on high.
In every hue, in every sway,
Whispers of petals dance and play.

The bees hum low, in rhythmic cheer,
Gathering nectar where dreams appear.
Every drop a wish on the breeze,
Nurtured by hope, carried through trees.

So wander freely, let your heart glean,
The magic alive in this floral sheen.
For whispers of petals cradle the night,
In dreams interwoven, pure and light.

Dreamscapes of the Whispering Woods

In whispering woods, where shadows sleep,
Dreamscapes awaken, secrets to keep.
The path winds gently, through moss and stone,
Each rustling leaf a tale of its own.

Where ancient trees guard the stories old,
And every bough has a memory told.
The wind carries echoes, soft and low,
Luring the wanderers, beckoning slow.

Fireflies linger, a soft-lit glow,
Guiding the way where enchantments flow.
Under the canopy, starlight weaves,
A tapestry spun from the dreams we believe.

In twilight's cradle, a magic hum,
A symphony played by the night's soft drum.
Draw near, dear traveler, let the woods imbue,
Your heart with the wonder the moonlight knew.

So dance 'neath the stars, let your spirit roam,
In dreamscapes of woods, may you find your home.
For in every rustle and sigh from the trees,
A world lies waiting, alive with mysteries.